My Coloring Book

For Adults and Teen-agers

By M.O.R.E. Publishers

My Coloring Book

Contributors:

Terry L. Holt

Melvin UpChurch

Barry C. Wilkins

http://morepublishers.biz
http://cafepress.com/MOREPublishers
www.ArtistRising.com/galleries/holtupchurchandwilkins

http:/createspace.com

978-0-9830325-9-5 (November 2016)

M.O.R.E. Publishers CO

Memphis, Tennessee

My Coloring Book

"UnNatural Hood"

Unnatural Hood! (Chapter 1)

By Terry Holt

From the sky, the area that was once our neighborhood had now resembled what could be compared to a junkyard! Fires were across every other block. Some of them were at the conjunctions of the four-way stop signs, while others stood in shambles of old smothering heaps. They now were unoccupied semi-structures that held the material of our days of old and youth. There wasn't very much food available, so daily.... almost 60% of time was spent scheming on how to successfully curve the ever- present sensations of hunger and thirst.

My Coloring Book

The sun to some of us in then-o-day could kill you if over-exposed. You barely had enough moisture to sweat, let alone travel over intense periods of day. So many years of neglecting the tactics of sustenance had cost humanity gravely millions of hours in front of the television, the thousands of days before the video games and what-not.

The basements here and there provided the best of the shelters. These were kept intensely clean because the sick and dying were present. Sometimes our dear friends would get well enough, while others - they'd fade away to death. They probably weren't too upset about the situation. There was nothing to do at day nor was there anymore whilst night.

There were no guarantees that the angels would come back for us at all. Who could deal with us? We started to think within ourselves. In the present state of mind.... we were all next to non-existence.

www.MOREPublishers.biz

My Coloring Book

"Twelve Again"

My Coloring Book

From the book **Twelve Again**

About the Artist

The art that you may have seen comes from being in constant atmospheres that are either too dangerous to relax properly, or on another note, too joyful to sit over extended periods of time. The pictures start with light lead. Afterward comes an intensely supervised microscopic ink stretch-out.

Since I've been with the colors, my pictures have taken on new dimensions, as if you would have to touch it to see where the surface started. These images take lots of time to shape. Some of them completely absorb me – taking my strictest attention. I only pray that the people that may have interest would take the many minutes necessary to examine every centimeter. In doing so, you'll see me there as well – just my way of waving hello!

Terry Holt

*Melvin UpChurch is a native of Memphis, Tennessee

*Barry C. Wilkins is a native of Marshall County, Mississippi.

Selections use are from works included in other authors' writings and drawn by the artists.

My Coloring Book

"The Dog"

My Coloring Book

"The Lady"

My Coloring Book

"The Cup"

My Coloring Book

"My Angel"

My Coloring Book

"The Bee"

My Coloring Book

"The Clown"

My Coloring Book

A TEAR FROM THE
CORNER OF HER EYE

Poetry and Essays by
ANNETTE ELOISE RILEY JOSEPH

My Coloring Book

"The Country Rooster"

My Coloring Book

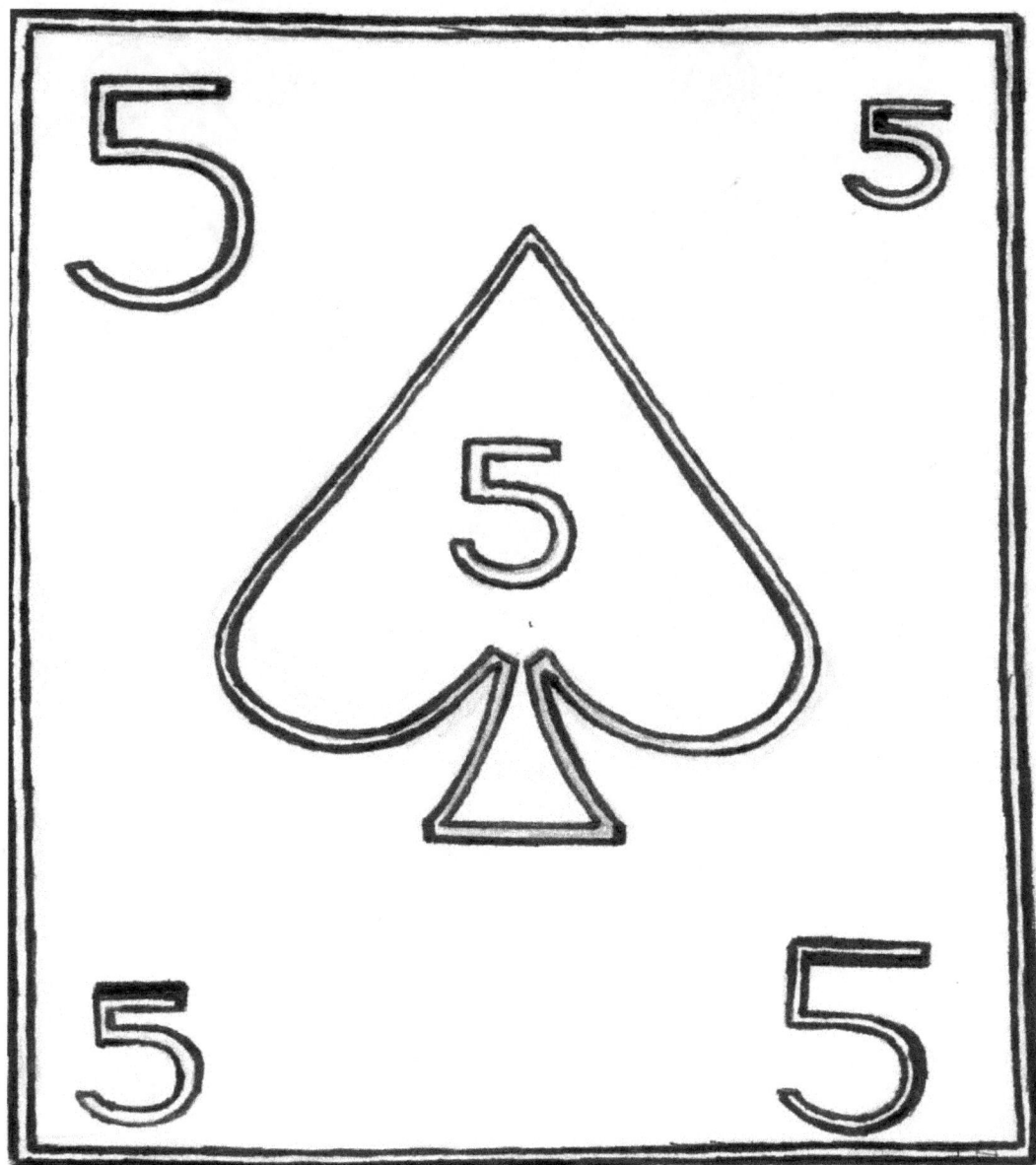

"The Spade"

My Coloring Book

XIAOTING PAINE
by
Billy Acy Neal

"The Guitar Player"

My Coloring Book

"The Gambler"

My Coloring Book

"The Multi-colored Bird"

My Coloring Book

"An Eagle"

My Coloring Book

"Family"

From Poems and Praise by Gertrude R. Anderson

My Coloring Book

"Liquid Virgin"

My Coloring Book

"Love"

From <u>Poems and Praise</u> by Gertrude R. Anderson

My Coloring Book

"The Mirror"

My Coloring Book

"History"

From <u>Poems and Praise</u> by Gertrude R. Anderson

My Coloring Book

The Bird

My Coloring Book

"Multi-colored Perch"

My Coloring Book

"The Woman"

My Coloring Book

"The Butterfly"

My Coloring Book

My Coloring Book

My Coloring Book

"The Girl"

My Coloring Book